EXPLORING WORLD CULTURES

Canada

Sharon Gordon

Cavendish Square

New York

This book is dedicated to my family, my husband, children and grandchildren, all of whom bring me great joy and purpose. And also to my brothers and sisters, who have been steady friends throughout my life.

Published in 2016 by Cavendish Square Publishing, LLC
243 5th Avenue, Suite 136, New York, NY 10016

Library of Congress Cataloging-in-Publication Data

Gordon, Sharon.
Canada / Sharon Gordon.
pages cm. — (Exploring world cultures)
Includes bibliographical references and index.
ISBN 978-1-50260-586-3 (hardcover) ISBN 978-1-50260-585-6 (paperback) ISBN 978-1-50260-587-0 (ebook)
1. Canada—Juvenile literature. I. Title.

F1008.2.G67 2015
971—dc23

2015002296

Editorial Director: David McNamara
Editor: Kristen Susienka
Copy Editor: Cynthia Roby
Art Director: Jeffrey Talbot
Designer: Joseph Macri
Senior Production Manager: Jennifer Ryder-Talbot
Production Editor: Renni Johnson
Photo Research: J8 Media

The photographs in this book are used by permission and through the courtesy of: LWA/Dann Tardif/Blend Images/Getty Images, cover; Karamysh/Shutterstock.com, 5; Rainer Lesniewski/Shutterstock.com, 6; Time Life Pictures/Mansell/The LIFE Picture Collection/Getty Images, 8; Derek R. Audette/Shutterstock.com, 10; James Wheeler/Shutterstock.com, 12; Alan Majchrowicz/Stone/Getty Images, 14; Yvette Cardozo/Photolibrary/Getty Images, 17; Deymos.HR/Shutterstock.com, 18; Sergei Bachlakov/Shutterstock.com, 20; Brent Lewin/Bloomberg via Getty Images, 22; Hans-Peter Merten/Robert Harding World Imagery/Getty Images, 24; Claus Andersen/Getty Images, 26; Sjschen/File:Original PoutineLaBanquise.jpg/Wikimedia Commons, 29.

Printed in the United States of America

Contents

Introduction

In 1535, an explorer named Jacques Cartier traveled to North America. He named the land "Canada," after hearing the Native people call it "Kanata," meaning "village." In 1867, Canada became the country's official name.

Water, ice, and wind have shaped Canada. Few people can live in its wild and cold places. Canada has many rivers, prairies, lakes, and tall mountains.

Canadian people are as different as the land. French Canadians remember customs of France. British Canadians celebrate customs of Great Britain. Native Canadians, or First Nations, live as they did in the past. With all their differences, Canadians are still united.

The beaver is Canada's national symbol. It is pictured on stamps and coins. Like Canadians, the beaver works hard. Bad weather cannot stop it from getting a job done.

Canada is a great place to live in and explore.

The beautiful Rocky Mountains have steep, snowcapped peaks.

Canada is one of the world's largest countries.

Canada is the second-largest country in the world. It borders the Atlantic, Pacific, and Arctic Oceans. It is made up of ten **provinces** and three **territories**.

The Northern Lights

In Canada, sometimes strange dancing lights light up the night sky. The lights are called the Northern Lights, or aurora borealis. They can be blue, green, or red.

Canada is beautiful but cold. **Tundra** in the far north is frozen all year long. Many provinces have warm summers and cold winters.

The Canadian Rockies in the west are very tall and get a lot of snow. Near the Pacific Ocean are the smaller Coast Mountains. Many islands dot the sea. In the east are the Appalachian Mountains. Many visitors come to see Niagara Falls, the world's largest waterfall.

FACT!

Canada has many large animals, including polar bears, moose, and wolves.

Canada belonged to Great Britain for many years, but in the 1800s people wanted more freedom. On July 1, 1867, Canada became the Dominion of Canada. Canada gained more power. John MacDonald became the country's first prime minister.

The Canadian Pacific Railway once connected Canada's coasts.

Old Quebec City

The beautiful stone walls of Old Quebec once kept it safe.

Over many years, other provinces were added to Canada. British Columbia joined in 1871 when railroads were being built, connecting everyone in the country. The last province to join was Newfoundland, in 1949. At this time, Great Britain was still in control.

The **Constitution** Act was passed in 1982. Basic rights were given to all Canadians. They could make changes to their laws without British approval.

Quebec never signed the 1982 Constitution. They wanted to become a separate nation. Many people in Quebec still feel this way.

FACT!

In 1886, Canada's east and west coasts were finally connected by a railroad.

The Parliament Buildings National Historic Site, where the federal government meets

Canada has its own government. Ottawa, in Ontario, is Canada's capital city. The provinces have more power than the territories. They can make their own local laws.

Parliament makes Canada's national laws. Members of the House of Commons are elected by the people. They write new laws. Members of the Senate are chosen. They review new laws.

The prime minister of Canada is selected by the House of Commons. He is the head of the government. He makes sure the laws are followed. He works with the Governor General, who speaks for the British government.

Canada also has a system of courts. They make sure the laws that are passed are fair.

Canadian Flag

One of Canada's national symbols is the maple leaf. It appears on the Canadian flag.

Logging is an important industry in Canada.

Canada is a leader in world trade. Wood from its forests becomes lumber and paper. Much of it is sold to other countries.

Many jobs depend on water. Ocean fishing is important on the coasts. Lakes and streams are important for freshwater fishing. Canada is a leader in **hydropower**. Water is used to make electricity.

Canada has a lot of oil and natural gas. They are used for heat and fuel. Some workers drill for them. Others get them ready to sell. Wheat and hay are grown on farms. Alberta has many cattle farms.

Most Canadians work for banks, stores, hotels, and restaurants. Montreal has many computer jobs. Canada's economy is important to the rest of the world.

The Loonie

Canada's one-dollar coin is called a "loonie." It shows a common loon, a Canadian bird.

Canada's environment is important to the people who live there. The First Nations of Canada used only what they needed. When the French

Banff National Park in Alberta has beautiful lakes and mountains.

and British arrived in the 1500s, they brought changes. They wanted to develop the resources, such as wood, fish, and animal furs. They sold furs around the world. Fishing became a business.

Banff National Park

In 1885, Banff, in Alberta, became home to Canada's first national park.

Today, Canadians protect the land and wildlife. There are forty-two national parks. **Marine** life is also protected.

Loggers are careful about how they take down trees. Businesses are careful not to pollute Canada's many freshwater lakes and streams. They are needed for safe drinking water.

The Trans-Canada Highway has free **charging stations** for electric cars. It is one of the world's first and longest "green" highways.

FACT!

Over two thousand miles of **pipeline** brings oil from Canada to the United States.

Canada is a huge country but its population is not. Less than 1 percent of the world's people live there.

Most Canadians are white. About half of the people are of British or French descent. In the Atlantic provinces, there are many people from Scotland and Ireland. The name Nova Scotia means "New Scotland."

FACT!

Many Cajun people living in the US state of Louisiana are descended from Acadians, a group of people who lived in Canada in the 1700s.

Today, people from other parts of the world have come to Canada to live a good life. Large cities are populated with many cultural groups.

The Underground Railroad

Many Canadians helped slaves use the Underground Railroad to escape from the Southern United States in the 1800s.

The Inuit people build igloos to survive in cold weather.

The earliest people of Canada are called the First Nations. The Inuit were once known as Eskimos. They still build igloos for hunting in the frozen north.

Lifestyle

Most Canadians live in large cities. They are near schools, stores, and jobs. The cities are modern and friendly.

Canadians like to be polite. They like to be on time. They are helpful to older people and people with **disabilities**.

Tourists visit Canada every year.

FACT!

The largest mall in North America is in Alberta.

Metric System

Canadians measure items using the **metric system.** Someone who is 4 feet tall is said to be 1.22 meters tall.

Weather is always on the minds of Canadians. In the winter it is very snowy. They check the forecast often.

Most Canadians drive their cars to work. Others use the bus, subway, train, or ferry. Some walk to work or ride a bike. Women are treated fairly at their jobs. They are respected by other workers.

In their free time, families watch TV, go shopping, or visit with friends. Parents and children stay in touch by using computers and cell phones.

Religion

Most Canadians are Christian. Among them, half are Roman Catholic. Most Catholics are French. Many live in Quebec. Other Christians are Protestant. The United Church of Canada and

People from many different cultu and religions live in Canada.

the Anglican Church of Canada are the largest Protestant groups.

FACT!

Inuit believe that all things are alive and have spirits. They sing and tell stories about them.

Christmas and Easter are official holidays. Throughout Canada, Christmas is celebrated with sparkling lights and decorations. Children find presents under the Christmas tree.

The Multicultural Act of 1985

This law encourages all people to respect other races and religions.

People who have come from different countries have brought new religions to Canada. Today there are groups of Jews, Muslims, Hindus, Sikhs, and Buddhists.

Some Canadians do not have a religion. Younger Canadians are less religious than older ones. It is okay to choose to follow a religion or not.

Language

Many signs in Canada are written in both French and English.

Both English and French are official languages in Canada. Most people speak English. Laws must be written in both. All talk in Parliament must be heard in both. Food labels must be written in both. Often Canadians add a "u" to words. They might spell color "colour" or neighbor "neighbour." They sometimes add "eh" to the ends of their sentences.

Chesterfield

A couch or sofa might be called a chesterfield.

In Quebec, French is the language of the streets. All signs are written in French and English. Children must learn French in school.

There are three main languages of the First Nations. The language of the Inuit is called Inuktitut.

More people are coming from Africa and Asia to the larger cities. They bring new languages to Canada. Many people today are also learning how to speak Chinese.

FACT!

Around 17.5 percent of Canadian people speak two languages.

23

Arts and Festivals

Different areas of Canada have their own kinds of music and art. In places such as Nova Scotia and Ontario, people enjoy Irish and Scottish songs and customs. They also like going to plays, movies, and festivals.

The world's greatest rodeo is held each year in Stampede Park in Calgary.

FACT!

Each year in Stratford, Ontario, a festival to celebrate the plays of William Shakespeare is held.

The Calgary **Stampede** is known all over the world. For ten days in July the streets in Calgary, Alberta, fill with cowboys and cowgirls. Visitors get free breakfast and cowboy hats. The whole town is filled with live music and cookouts.

On July 1, Canadians celebrate the birth of their country. Big cities hold special festivities, such as fireworks.

The Quebec Winter Carnival celebrates ice and snow. Visitors can see a huge palace made of ice. Families enjoy night parades.

Royal Canadian Mounted Police

In warm months, the Royal Canadian Mounted Police, also called Mounties, ride their horses in parades across the country.

Fun and Play

There is much to see and do in Canada. Sports are very popular. Lacrosse is the official sport of summer. Ice hockey is the official sport of winter. A popular hockey team is the Toronto Maple

Canadians love to watch their favor[ite] hockey teams.

Leafs. In the summer, many people also watch baseball or soccer.

The long winters and large mountains are good for skiing and snowboarding. Curling is also fun to play in the winter.

Lacrosse

Lacrosse was first played in Canada by the First Nations.

Canada's forests and lakes bring many visitors. Hikers enjoy the beautiful trails. The lakes are good for fishing and boating.

Canadians visit their many beautiful national parks. They also like going to the zoo. The Toronto Zoo is the largest zoo in Canada.

FACT!

Winnie-the-Pooh was based on a Canadian black bear cub living at the London Zoo. A little boy named Christopher Robin loved to visit him.

Food

Canadians usually have three meals a day. Dinner is the last and largest meal. It is usually eaten with family after work or school.

Giant Lobster

The largest lobster was caught in Nova Scotia in 1977. It weighed more than 44 pounds (20 kilograms).

Canada is filled with lakes and **glaciers**. It is easy to find a bottle of "Glacier fresh" water.

Maple syrup is everywhere! Canadians put it on their pancakes. They also put it in their cookies, candies, and treats.

Some Canadian foods are not very healthy. Poutine are French fries covered with gravy and cheese. Canadians also enjoy potato chips. Ketchup chips taste like ketchup. Other chips taste like pickles.

Ginger ale is a soft drink that was invented by a Toronto doctor in 1919. Today, Canada Dry is sold all over the world.

Quebec gave Canada one of its favorite fast foods—poutine!

FACT!

The popular café chain Tim Hortons started in Hamilton, Ontario, Canada, in 1964.

Glossary

charging station	A place where cars that run on electricity get more power.
Constitution	The basic laws of Canada.
disabilities	Health problems that keep people from doing everyday things.
glacier	Thick ice that moves.
hydropower	Power that comes from falling water.
marine	Of the sea.
metric system	A way of measuring objects by height and weight.
pipeline	A long pipe for moving something.
province	A section of a country that has its own education system and environmental laws.
stampede	A large rush of animals.
territory	An area that belongs to a government.
tundra	Frozen, flat land.

Find Out More

Books

Bowers, Vivien. *Wow Canada!* Toronto: Maple Tree Press Inc., 2010.

McDonnell, Ginger. *Next Stop: Canada*. TIME for Kids: Nonfiction Readers. Huntington Beach, CA: Teacher Created Materials, 2011.

Websites

Canada's Treasure Trek

www.tvokids.com/games/canadastreasuretrek

The Canadian Geographic/Atlas of Canada

www.canadiangeographic.ca/kids/default.asp

Video

The Providences and Territories of Canada

www.youtube.com/watch?v=vmdBJpwTrn4

Discover the provinces and territories of Canada, along with their capitals, industries, and geography.

Index

About the Author

Sharon Gordon has been writing children's books for many years. She has written science and nature books for many companies. Sharon was born and raised in the United States. For fun, Sharon likes to travel. When she is not writing, she loves spending time with her family.